G000154363

BREAKFAST WITH Mrs BEETON

HEARTY FARE

BREAKFAST WITH Mrs BEETON

HEARTY FARE

WARD LOCK

First published 1990 by Ward Lock
Villiers House, 41/47 Strand, London WC2N 5JE, England

A Cassell imprint

British Library Cataloguing in Publication Data
Beeton, Mrs, *1836-1865*
Breakfast with Mrs. Beeton.
1. Breakfasts – Recipes
I. Title
000.00

ISBN 0-7063-6889-4

Designed by Cherry Randell
Illustrations by Mike Shoebridge
Edited by Alison Leach and Helen Douglas-Cooper

Typeset in Goudy Old Style by Litho Link Ltd, Welshpool, Powys, Wales

Printed and bound in Italy by Olivotto

Contents

INTRODUCTION

During the Middle Ages, breakfast consisted of bread, boiled beef, mutton, salt herring, wine and ale, and it was eaten at any time between getting up and noon. By the seventeenth century, these haphazard eating patterns had become more ordered. Breakfast was taken shortly after rising, and was followed by dinner at midday and supper in the early evening. Breakfast was a relatively light affair and the foods eaten depended largely on what was left over from the day before. There was usually a selection of cold meats, bread, cheese, cakes and butter, ale and claret. Tea, coffee and chocolate gradually took over from alcoholic drinks, tea becoming the most popular. By the eighteenth century the first meal of the day was generally eaten between 9 and 10 o'clock, and nothing else was eaten until dinner at 2 or 3 in the afternoon.

During the nineteenth century the time stayed the same, but the meal became much more substantial, particularly for men, who ate steaks, pork chops, eggs and cold meats as well as toast and rolls. Ladies tended to take a lighter meal of toast or hot, sweet rolls with chocolate, coffee or tea. The breakfast table was laid with a white linen cloth and napkins, good china, silver pots and dishes, and decorations of flowers or fruit. Pots of freshly made chocolate, tea or coffee were placed in front of a large urn, and at the head of the table were the cups and saucers, coffee cups to the right and tea cups to the left. There was also a slop basin for the dregs, jugs of cold milk, hot milk and cream, toast

racks full of freshly toasted bread and a wooden platter with a new loaf fresh from the oven. Hot rolls were wrapped in napkins, and on the sideboard was arranged a large selection of hot and cold dishes.

The rapid developments in industry and commerce during the Victorian period brought ever-increasing wealth to the middle classes, and families could afford to eat well. Men who had to be in their offices by nine o'clock needed a hearty breakfast before starting their working day, and by the 1860s the usual time for breakfast was 8 o'clock. The huge spread laid out in the breakfast or dining-room included cold joints, fresh and potted meats and fish, cold game and poultry, veal and ham pies, game pies, cold ham and pressed tongue, hot, broiled mackerel, mutton chops, steaks, kidneys, sausages, bacon and eggs, muffins, toast, marmalade, tea, chocolate and coffee, and, in summer, a selection of fresh fruit.

Today we have become more aware of the need to eat less cholesterol and fewer calories, and we often start the day with only fruit juice or cereal and toast. It is a great treat, though, once in a while, and especially at weekends, to indulge in the delicious traditional dishes that Mrs Beeton included in her cookery books.

DRINKS

Individual tastes in early morning drinks vary greatly. For many people a glass of fruit juice is the first drink of the day. To follow, choose between the burst of caffeine that coffee gives, the more gently stimulating effect of tea, or the soothing, warming qualities of a cup of hot chocolate.

MAKING COFFEE

Saucepan method

Heat the measured quantity of medium-ground coffee and water in a saucepan and bring almost to boiling point. Remove from the heat and stir; then cover and leave to stand for a few minutes. Strain into a warm jug and serve at once.

Filter method

Place a filter paper in a small conical strainer unless the coffee pot has a built-in filter. Warm the jug and measure fine-ground coffee into the filter which is placed on top of the jug. Pour on freshly boiling water and allow the water to drip through the coffee and filter into the jug below; do not pour too much water into the filter at once. Electric filter systems often have automatic timing devices. Follow the manufacturer's instructions.

Percolator method

Most percolators are sold with manufacturers' instructions for use. In general, add the required amount of water to the percolator, measure medium-ground coffee into the special container (the basket), insert into the percolator and put on the lid. Heat and percolate for 6–8 minutes only; then remove the coffee grounds in their container, and serve. As with the filter method, electric percolators may have automatic timing devices.

Vacuum method

These appliances have a lower glass

TO MAKE PERFECT COFFEE

The best and preferred way to draw the full flavour from ground coffee beans is by infusion, and there are many different infusers on the market that are easy to use and that produce very good coffee. If, however, you do not have one of these, an earthenware or glass jug will do just as well. Silver, tinned or enamelled iron are also good, but avoid aluminium and plain iron as they will spoil the flavour of the coffee. Follow these rules and you will always make good coffee:

- Always use fresh beans of a good quality.
- Grind the beans immediately before use, or use freshly opened vacuum-packed ground beans.
- Fill the kettle with cold, freshly drawn water and leave to boil.
- Warm the pot first.
- Always make the coffee full-strength, allowing about 45 ml/3 tbsp of grounds to 600 ml (1 pint) of water. Vary to suit personal taste.
- Never pour boiling water on to the grounds as it will vapourize much of the essential flavour and extract bitter-tasting chemicals. Use water that is just under boiling point.
- Drink the coffee hot. If you need to reheat it, do not boil, but heat gently in a bain-marie, double saucepan, or on low power in a microwave oven for a few minutes.

bowl in which water is heated, and an upper bowl in which fine-ground coffee is placed. When the water in the lower bowl comes to boiling point, it rises up into the upper bowl. Stir and leave on a low heat for 2–3 minutes; then remove from the heat and the coffee will filter back into the lower bowl. Remove the upper bowl and serve.

Espresso method

Water is added to the lower container of a vacuum-type coffee maker; high-roast, fine-ground coffee is measured into a basket, and the upper container, with the basket, is screwed into the lower container. When heated, the water rises under pressure and is forced through the coffee; this extracts more flavour than the other methods. When all the water has risen into the upper container, it is removed from the heat and the coffee served.

Quantities

For roasted, ground coffee of average strength, use about 30 ml/2 tbsp of coffee per 500 ml/ 17 fl oz water, depending on the flavour of the beans, the fineness of the grind, and the method used to make the drink. Use slightly less Brazilian or Jamaican coffee than Kenyan.

Serving coffee

Milk can be served with coffee, either hot or cold. If heated, be careful not to let it boil as it will then spoil the flavour of the coffee. If serving coffee with cream, use single or whipping cream.

MAKING TEA

Quantities

Allow 5 ml/1 tsp per person and 1 extra, ie for 2 people, allow 3 × 5 ml spoons/3 tsp and for 4 people, allow 5 × 5 ml spoons/ 5 tsp. If using tea bags in a pot, allow 1 per person and 1 extra. For instant tea, use 5 ml/1 tsp per cup.

Leaf tea

First bring the water to the boil; just before it boils, pour a little water into the pot to warm it, rinse out, and throw away. Put the required quantity of tea in the pot. When the water boils, pour it over the tea. It is essential that the water is boiling up to the moment it is poured over the tea, or the flavour of the tea will be spoiled and there will be small tea leaves floating on top. Stir the tea once, then leave to infuse for 5 minutes; stir once more, then strain into cups. If milk is used, it can be added to the cups before the tea or afterwards.

Tea bags and instant tea

If using tea bags, make as above, remembering to stir the tea before serving to extract the maximum flavour. It is not necessary to use a strainer for this method.

Use instant tea according to directions on packet.

Herbal teas or tisanes
Make tisanes in exactly the same way as ordinary tea, and leave to infuse for 5–10 minutes. If using dried herbs, allow, as a general rule, 5 ml/1 tsp per person and 1 extra, but when using fresh herbs, allow 3 × 5 ml spoons/3 tsp and 1 extra. Fresh herbs should be bruised before being put in the pot to extract the maximum flavour.

MOCHA CHOCOLATE

25 ml/5 tsp instant coffee powder
15 ml/1 tbsp drinking chocolate powder
few grains of salt
500 ml/17 fl oz milk
250 ml/8 fl oz water
50 g/2 oz grated chocolate

Mix together the instant coffee, drinking chocolate, and salt in a bowl. Add a little milk and mix the powders to a smooth paste.

Put the remaining milk and the water into a small saucepan, and stir in the paste. Heat to just below boiling point.

Pour into warmed glasses or mugs, and sprinkle the grated chocolate on top before serving.

SERVES 4

BUCKS FIZZ

juice of 4 oranges
chilled dry champagne

Strain the orange juice and chill it. Divide it between four champagne glasses and top up with the champagne. Do not add ice.

SERVES 4

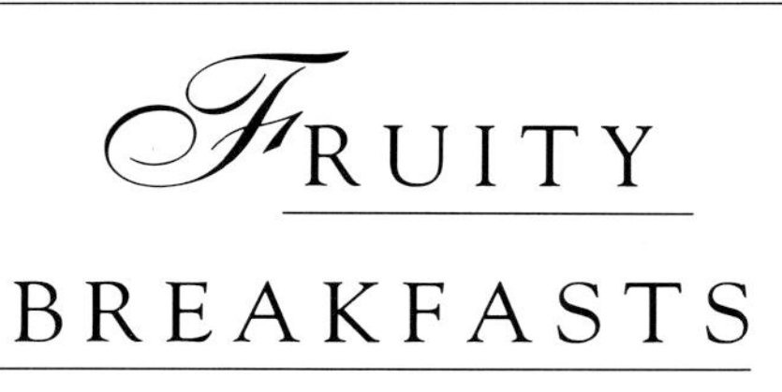

FRUITY BREAKFASTS

Fresh fruit juices, compôtes and cocktails give the body valuable vitamins and minerals, while dried fruits are high in the fibre which the digestive system needs. They make a very refreshing way to start the day.

GRAPEFRUIT

2 large firm grapefruit
white **or** *brown sugar*
40 ml/8 tsp medium-dry sherry (optional)

Decoration
2 maraschino **or** *glacé cherries*
angelica (optional)

Choose sound, ripe fruit and wipe them. Cut them in half crossways, and remove the pips. Snip out the cores with scissors.

With a stainless steel knife (preferably with a saw edge) or a grapefruit knife, cut round each half between the flesh and the pith to loosen the flesh. Cut between the membranes which divide the segments, but leave the flesh in the halved skins as if uncut.

Sweeten to taste with sugar, or, if preferred, pour 10 ml/2 tsp sherry over each half grapefruit, and serve sugar separately. Decorate the centre of each half fruit with a halved cherry and with pieces of angelica, if liked.

Chill before serving. Serve one half fruit per person.

SERVES 4

DRIED FRUIT COMPÔTE

100 g/4 oz dried apricots
100 g/4 oz prunes
100 g/4 oz dried figs
50 g/2 oz dried apple rings
30 ml /2 tbsp clear honey
2.5 cm/ 1 inch piece of cinnamon stick
2 cloves
pared rind and juice of ½ lemon
50 g/2 oz raisins
50 g/2 oz flaked almonds, toasted

Combine the apricots, prunes, and figs in a bowl. Add water to cover and leave to soak. Put the apples in a separate bowl with water to cover and leave both bowls to soak overnight.

Next day, place the honey in saucepan with 600 ml/1 pint water. Add the cinnamon stick, cloves and lemon rind. Bring to the boil. Stir in the lemon juice.

Drain both bowls of soaked fruit. Add the mixed fruit to the pan, cover and simmer for 10 minutes. Stir in the drained apples and simmer for 10 minutes more, then add the raisins and simmer for 2–3 minutes. Discard the cinnamon, cloves and lemon rind.

Spoon the compôte into a serving dish and sprinkle with the almonds. Serve warm or cold, with fresh cream.

STEWED OR POACHED FRESH FRUIT

Fruit can be poached or stewed. If poached, it is cooked in a syrup or other liquid at just below boiling point. The water should just shiver. If stewed, it is cooked at a slightly higher heat in a covered pan.

The syrup is made from sugar and water, or other liquid, with extra flavouring sometimes added. The quantities of sugar and water will depend on the sweetness and ripeness of the fruit; those given below are only rough guides. To make the syrup, put the sugar and liquid into a large saucepan with any solid flavouring. Bring to the boil, reduce the heat, and simmer for 3–4 minutes. Skim and serve as required.

The fruit can be cooked either in a saucepan over a direct gentle heat or in a casserole in a moderate to cool oven. The second method takes longer but preserves the shape of the fruit better. The time taken depends on the type of fruit, its size, and ripeness. Most cook in 20 minutes or less in a saucepan, but take twice as long in a casserole. Use a stainless steel, aluminium or enamelled pan or an earthenware casserole. It is not advisable to use copper or brass.

When the fruit is cooked, remove it with a perforated spoon, drain well, and transfer to a serving bowl. Discard any solid flavourings from the syrup and boil until it is well reduced. Pour it over the fruit and serve either hot or cold.

Apples and pears: Peel, core, and leave whole if small, quarter if large. Make a syrup with 100 g/4 oz sugar and 250 ml/8 fl oz water (more if the fruit is very hard) per 500 g/18 oz fruit. Flavour with lemon rind, cloves or cinnamon stick. Colour the syrup with cochineal, if liked, or replace some of the water with white wine or cider. Put the prepared fruit into the liquid immediately to preserve its colour; it must be completely covered by the liquid. Stew either in a saucepan or in a casserole in a moderate oven. Cooking pears may take 4–5 hours in the oven.

Peaches and apricots: Peel, stone, and halve or quarter the fruit, depending on its size. Make a syrup with 100 g/4 oz sugar and 250 ml/8 fl oz water per 500 g/18 oz fruit. Flavour with almond or vanilla essence or with a few kernels from the fruit stones. Replace some of the water with white wine if liked.

Plums, greengages, and damsons: Wash the fruit, remove the stalks, and the stones if liked. Make a syrup with 100 g/4 oz sugar and 250 ml/8 fl oz water per 500 g/18 oz fruit. Flavour with lemon rind, cloves, cinnamon stick, or with a few kernels from the fruit stones. Replace some of the water with red wine, for red plums, if liked. Stew either in a saucepan or in a casserole in a moderate oven.

CEREALS

Cereals of all types are excellent for breakfast as they stave off hunger, help the body to generate inner warmth and provide essential fibre. Those who are concerned about calories should be careful about the amount of sugar that is added, both by the manufacturer and sugar from the breakfast bowl.

MUESLI

1 large dessert apple
unstrained fresh lemon juice
100 g/4 oz rolled oats
15 g/½ oz wheat bran
25 g/1 oz sultanas
25 g/1 oz seedless raisins
25 g/1 oz clear honey **or** *soft light brown sugar*
250 ml/8 fl oz natural yoghurt
25 g/1 oz chopped mixed nuts

Core and dice the apple without peeling. Put in a bowl and toss immediately in the lemon juice. Set aside.

Mix together the oats, bran, sultanas, and raisins in a bowl. Warm the honey, if used. Stir the honey or sugar into the muesli mixture. Drain off the lemon juice and add the apple.

Serve in four individual bowls, cover with the yoghurt, and sprinkle with the nuts.

If liked, 25–50 g/1–2 oz chopped dates or dried apricots can be added with the sultanas, or 50 g/2 oz chopped fresh fruit can be added with the apple.

SERVES 4

HONESTY PUDDING

50 g/2 oz fine oatmeal
15 ml/1 tbsp plain flour
750 ml/1¼ pints milk
1 egg
pinch of salt
2.5 ml/½ tsp grated orange rind
fat for greasing

Grease a 750 ml/1¼ pint pie dish. Set the oven at 180°C/350°F/gas 4.

Blend the oatmeal and flour to a smooth paste in a bowl with a little of the milk. Bring the remaining milk to the boil in a saucepan, and pour it over the oatmeal mixture, stirring all the time.

Return the mixture to the pan and cook over a low heat for 5 minutes, stirring all the time. Remove from the heat, and leave to cool for 5 minutes.

Beat the egg until liquid, and then beat it into the cooled oatmeal mixture. Flavour with the salt and orange rind.

Pour the mixture into the prepared pie dish, and bake for 35–40 minutes.

Serve hot from the dish, with cream and brown sugar.

SERVES 4

PORRIDGE

900 ml/1½ pints water
150 g/5 oz rolled oats (not quick cooking)
salt
demerara sugar **or** *golden syrup (optional)*

Bring the water to a fast boil in a heavy saucepan. Sprinkle in the oats gradually, stirring with a wooden spoon. Reduce the heat, cover the pan and leave to simmer for 8 minutes.

Add salt to taste, cover, and leave to simmer for another 8 minutes or until the porridge is the required consistency.

Spoon into cold bowls (to stop the porridge cooking). Serve at once sprinkled either with extra salt or with demerara sugar or golden syrup. Add hot or cold milk to taste. Alternatively, top the porridge with a knob of fresh salted butter.

SERVES 4

OATMEAL PORRIDGE

1 litre/1¾ pints water
150 g/5 oz coarse **or** *fine oatmeal*
5 ml/1 tsp salt

Bring the water to the boil in a thick saucepan. Sprinkle in the oatmeal steadily, stirring all the time with a spurtle (porridge stick) or wooden spoon.

Cover the pan, reduce the heat, and simmer. Add the salt after 10 minutes. Cook for 20–30 minutes altogether.

Ladle into cold bowls or porringers and serve with a separate bowl of either cream, milk or buttermilk. Dip each spoonful of porridge into this before eating.

If the oatmeal is soaked in the water overnight, the cooking time is shortened.

SERVES 4

CREE'D WHEAT

375 g/13 oz hulled **or** *pearled wheat*
pinch of salt
about 2 litres/3½ pints water

Put the wheat into a heatproof container with the salt, and cover with the cold water. Leave to steep in a very warm place for 24–36 hours, until the starch grains have become a soft mass.

The container can be put in the plate-warming drawer of an oven or on a radiator or boiler. Add extra water during steeping, if the grains absorb it all.

Pour off any excess water, and put the grains in a saucepan. Stir over a very gentle heat until the mixture boils and becomes a glutinous mass. Leave to cool, and use in the recipe for Frumenty (page 18).

MAKES 450 g/1 lb

FRUMENTY

450 g/1 lb cree'd wheat (page 18)
75–100 g/3–4 oz currants **or** *seedless raisins*
300–500 ml/10–17 fl oz milk
15ml/1 tbsp plain flour (optional)
sugar, honey **or** *treacle*
ground allspice **or** *cinnamon* **or** *grated nutmeg*

Prepare the cree'd wheat.

Meanwhile, soak the dried fruit

in enough water to cover; leave until soft and swollen.

Put the cree'd wheat into a saucepan with the milk. Drain the dried fruit and add to the cree'd wheat. Stir over a gentle heat until the mixture comes to the boil and is thick and creamy.

Thicken the mixture, if liked, by blending the flour to a cream with a little cold milk and stirring it into the hot frumenty. Sweeten and flavour to taste.

Serve hot like porridge, with a knob of butter on each helping, or with cream and rum.

SERVES 6–8

FRUMENTY

Frumenty is probably the oldest recorded English dish, and was originally served as an accompaniment to meats such as porpoise and venison, certainly in the Middle Ages and probably before that. It is so called because it is made from fermented wheat. New hulled or pearled wheat (wheat with the first husk removed) is steeped in water and then left on a low heat overnight until it forms a stiff, glutinous jelly called cree'd wheat. Traditionally, this was then mixed with sugar, milk or cream or ale and a little flour to thicken it, and in this simple form it was eaten as a breakfast pottage. For festive occasions spices, egg yolks, honey and dried fruits were added, and sometimes claret or rum. It was eaten in the south of England at such times as harvest, hallowe'en, Christmas Eve, New Year, Mid-Lent and Easter, while in the north it was more commonly a Christmas dish. Very often a dish was placed outside the front door for the pharisees (fairies).

Flummery is similar to frumenty but is made from cree'd oatmeal instead of wheat. The term 'flummery' is sometimes used for any starch jelly made from wheat flour, rice, ground rice, barley, sago or potatoes.

COOKED BREAKFASTS

Few people have time for full cooked breakfasts during a busy working week, but at weekends or on holiday mornings the traditional dishes are a treat. These recipes are also excellent as part of a brunch or as a light meal at midday or in the evening.

DEVILLED KIDNEYS

4 sheep's **or** *8 lamb's kidneys*
30 ml/2 tbsp dripping **or** *oil*
15 ml/1 tbsp chopped onion
2.5 ml/½ tsp salt
1.25 ml/¼ tsp cayenne pepper
15 ml/1 tbsp chutney
10 ml/2 tsp lemon juice
2.5 ml/½ tsp prepared mustard
125 ml/4½ fl oz stock
2 egg yolks
soft white breadcrumbs

Skin the kidneys, cut them in half lengthways, and remove the cores; then cut them into neat pieces.

Heat the dripping or oil in a small frying pan, add the onion, and cook gently until softened but not browned. Add the kidney, salt, cayenne pepper, chutney, lemon juice, mustard, and stock.

Heat to boiling point, reduce the heat, cover the pan, and simmer gently for 15–20 minutes, until the kidney is cooked. Leave until slightly cooled.

Beat the egg yolks lightly and stir them into the kidney mixture. Sprinkle in enough breadcrumbs to make the mixture a soft consistency. Re-season if required.

Serve on buttered toast.

SERVES 4

GRILLED KIDNEYS

4 sheep's **or** *8 lamb's kidneys*
30 ml/2 tbsp butter
salt and pepper
4 slices of fried bread
chopped parsley
bacon rolls to garnish

Skin the kidneys, cut them in half lengthways, and remove the cores. Skewer them with small metal poultry skewers along their length to keep them flat.

Melt the butter, and brush a little on the cut sides of the kidneys. Place them on the grill rack, cut side up, and grill for 5–8 minutes, turning often, and basting with more butter if needed. When cooked through, remove the skewers carefully.

Season the kidneys well, and place them, cut side up, on the slices of fried bread. Sprinkle with chopped parsley, and garnish with bacon rolls.

SERVES 4

SETTING A BREAKFAST TRAY

When setting a tray it is important to put as much thought into the arrangement as when setting a table. Choose a tray that is big enough to allow plenty of space for all the necessary bits and pieces. Use either a colourful tray that co-ordinates with the décor of the bedroom, or decorate a less interesting one with an embroidered or lace tray-cloth. Arrange all the china and cutlery in the normal positions with a napkin on the left, folded prettily. A large napkin is best, as it will provide ample cover for bed linen and night clothes. On the right set a newspaper or magazine with any post that has arrived. Leave space for a tiny posy of flowers in a low vase, dainty egg cup or stylish glass, or simply lay a single flower on the napkin. For a sick child, use bright, novelty china, and cut toast or bread into interesting shapes. For an adult who is ill, use pastel shades for linens and china, and arrange small quantities of food carefully.

CODDLED EGGS

Coddled eggs are very soft-boiled eggs, with the whites soft and the yolks just set. Being easily digested, they are ideal for invalids.

Put the eggs into a saucepan of boiling water, cover with a lid, and remove from the heat, but keep the water hot without simmering for about 6 minutes for a small egg, and 8–9 minutes for large eggs.

Alternatively, put the eggs into a pan of cold water, bring slowly to the boil, and remove them immediately.

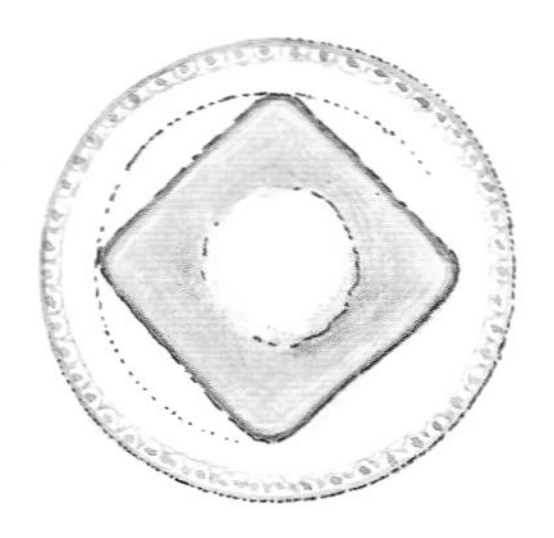

POACHED EGGS

To poach an egg perfectly needs careful attention. Do not try to poach very fresh or stale eggs as the yolks break easily.

Eggs can be poached in water, stock or milk. Water is the usual medium. The liquid should simmer, not boil, as the movement will break up the egg white.

Salt can be added to the water, to raise the temperature at which it simmers. A little vinegar or lemon juice can also be added to water or stock since the acid makes the egg white coagulate quickly and not break away from the yolk. Care must be taken when adding salt or acid, however, because too much will flavour the eggs.

Stock is used to poach an egg when extra flavour is wanted, but this flavour is delicate and should not be masked by a strongly flavoured accompaniment.

Eggs can be poached in milk when the liquid is required for making a sauce.

Put 5 cm/2 inches of the chosen liquid into a shallow pan and bring to simmering point. (Eggs are easier to remove from a shallow pan).

Break an egg into a cup or on to a saucer and slide the egg into the liquid, holding the cup or saucer near the surface of the liquid. If necessary, gather the white together gently with a spoon and roll the egg over after a few seconds. This gives a more compact shape to the poached egg.

Simmer gently, with the liquid hardly moving, for 2–3 minutes. Lift out the egg, using a perforated spoon or fish slice, and drain well. Blot on absorbent kitchen paper to remove any excess liquid before serving.

Provided the pan is big enough for them to cook without touching each other, 2 or 3 eggs can be poached at the same time.

More evenly shaped eggs can be produced by using plain pastry cutters as moulds. Put the required number of buttered 7.5 cm/3 inch cutters into the simmering liquid and break an egg into each. When the eggs are just set, remove the cutters and lift the eggs out, using a perforated spoon or fish slice.

Eggs can be poached in swirling water to give a neatly rounded shape. For this method, half fill a small pan with water, and when it is simmering, stir the water vigorously in one direction with a spoon. Slip the eggs into the centre of the whirlpool and the moving water should fold the white over the yolk.

If eggs are poached one at a time for serving together, slip each poached egg into a bowl of hand-hot water as soon as it is cooked to keep warm until they are all ready. If the eggs are wanted cold, put them straight into cold water after poaching, to prevent them toughening.

Cold poached eggs can be reheated in fairly hot water; but it must not be very hot or the eggs will harden. Leave for a few minutes to warm through, drain, and serve.

Eggs can also be poached in a special egg poacher, although technically speaking they are steamed. The poacher consists of a shallow container, shaped like a frying pan, which is half filled with water. A tray fits on top, holding 1–4 cups made from metal or other heat-resisting material, and is covered by a lid.

Put a small piece of butter into each cup, heat the pan and, when the water boils, break the eggs into the cups; season them lightly and cover with the lid.

Simmer gently for 3–5 minutes until the eggs are lightly set. Loosen them round the edge with a knife and lift them out on to a serving dish with a spoon.

SCRAMBLED EGGS

50 g/2 oz butter
8 eggs
salt and pepper
30–45 ml/2–3 tbsp top of the milk
or *single cream*

Melt the butter in a heavy-based frying or omelette pan. Beat the eggs, salt and pepper together lightly. Before the butter begins to sizzle, pour the eggs into the pan. Reduce the heat to very low.

Allow the eggs to set slightly round the sides and on the bottom of the pan. Then, using a wooden spoon or spatula, stir slowly and constantly. Run the spoon round the edge of the pan and draw the cooked egg in towards the centre. Draw the cooked egg up from the base of the pan.

When most of the egg has set, remove the pan from the heat at once. The eggs become dry and granulated or watery if they are overcooked. Add the milk or cream (which will stop any further cooking), and stir carefully until the eggs are evenly set into a soft, creamy mixture. Serve immediately.

Alternatively, 125 ml/4½ fl oz milk can be beaten in with the eggs and seasoning. Cook as above but do not add any milk or cream afterwards. Take particular care not to overcook the eggs using this method. Remove the pan from the heat while some of the egg is still liquid, since no cold milk is added to stop any further cooking.

SERVES 4

FRIED EGGS

Eggs can be either shallow-fried or deep-fried.

To shallow-fry, melt a little fat, dripping, lard, butter, bacon fat or cooking oil in a frying pan. Allow about 7.5 ml/1½ tsp per egg. The fat should be just hot, not sizzling.

Break the eggs, one at a time, into a cup or saucer and slide them carefully into the fat. Cook over a gentle heat for 2–3 minutes until the whites are no longer transparent; high heat toughens the egg whites and makes them crisp round the edges.

Lift the eggs out of the pan, using a fish slice or a broad palette knife. Hold for 1–2 seconds above the pan to allow any surplus fat to drain off before putting them on the serving dish or plate. Fried eggs can be blotted with absorbent kitchen paper to remove any excess fat.

If liked, the eggs can be basted with the hot fat during cooking, using a spoon or wooden spatula. This makes a film over the yolk, and cooks the top of the white more thoroughly. The egg is usually cooked in 1–2 minutes.

Some people prefer fried eggs which are turned over during cooking, so that both sides are fried. Fried eggs can be cooked in 1–2 minutes.

To deep-fry, half fill a small, deep pan with lard or oil. Heat it to 180°C/350°F (when a square of white bread sizzles immediately without browning) and then maintain this temperature.

Break one egg into a cup or saucer and slide it carefully into the fat. With a wooden spatula pull the white over the yolk so as to cover it completely. Turn the egg over in the oil.

The egg cooks very quickly, in 30–60 seconds from the moment it touches the fat. Have a perforated spoon ready and lift out the egg as soon as the white is set. Blot on absorbent kitchen paper to remove any excess fat, and serve immediately.

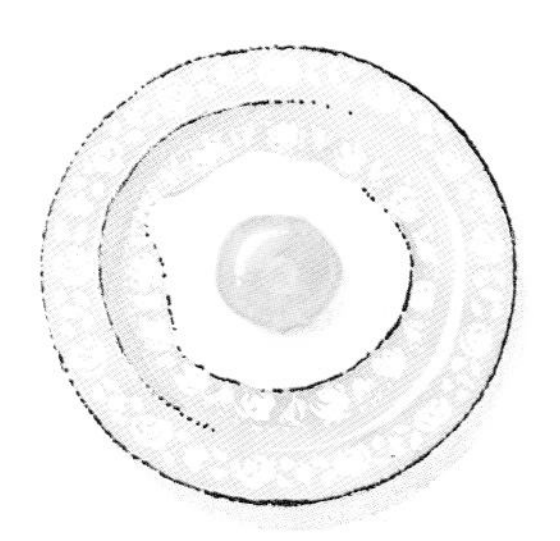

◇◆◇

PERFECT BOILED EGGS

Always use eggs that are as fresh as possible.

⁂ Have the eggs ready at room temperature.

⁂ Use just enough boiling water to cover the eggs.

⁂ Use a spoon to carefully and slowly lower each egg into the boiling water so that it does not crack against the side or bottom of the pan.

⁂ Ask each person how they like their egg, and time the cooking process carefully.

⁂ For a lightly boiled egg, allow 3 minutes
To set the white allow at least 3¾–4 minutes
For a slightly harder egg allow 6–7 minutes
For hard-boiled eggs allow 10 minutes

⁂ Very fresh eggs will take slightly longer than others.

⁂ Remove each egg carefully from the pan and place in an egg cup with an egg cosy over the top, or keep warm in a covered dish.

⁂ When hard-boiling eggs for salads or sandwich fillings, boil for 10 minutes, then drain and stand in cold, running water for several minutes to prevent the yolks from blackening.

◇◆◇

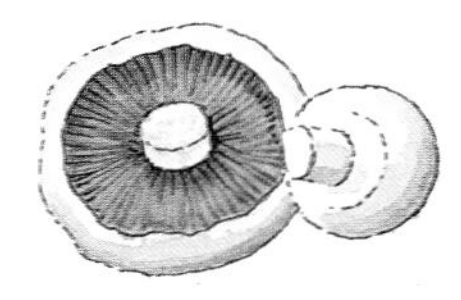

MUSHROOMS

Cultivated mushrooms are available throughout the year. There are three main types which are all grown from the same spore, the only difference being their age.

The youngest mushrooms are the small round button ones in which the underneath of the mushroom caps touches the stalks; cup mushrooms are slightly larger and flatter but still have a lip on the underside; the larger, flat mushrooms are the oldest and have the strongest flavour.

For pale-coloured sauces, it is always best to use button or cup mushrooms because the black underside of flat mushrooms will discolour a sauce.

Wild or field mushrooms are similar to cultivated mushrooms. They can be cooked in all the same ways and are particularly good grilled or stuffed.

Grilling is suitable for flat or large cup mushrooms. Remove the stalks; these can be put into the grill pan under the rack and will cook in the juices from the caps.

Brush both surfaces of the mushrooms with oil or dot with butter or margarine; season with salt and pepper.

Place the mushrooms on the rack of the grill pan and cook under a moderate grill for about 5 minutes or until the mushrooms are very tender, turning once, and basting with fat several times to prevent them drying out.

Serve with the juices collected in the grill pan.

To fry, for every 100 g/4 oz mushrooms, heat 25 g/1 oz butter, margarine, or lard, or 30 ml/2 tbsp oil in a frying pan.

Fry the mushrooms for about 5 minutes or until they are very tender. Season with salt and black pepper, preferably freshly ground. A squeeze of lemon juice also improves the flavour.

Serve together with the cooking liquid, sprinkled with chopped parsley, chives or lemon thyme.

COUNTRY HOUSE BREAKFAST

Dried fruit compôte
Porridge

Kippers
Bacon and eggs
Cumberland sausages
Devilled kidneys
Mushrooms
Fried bread

Oatmeal pancakes
Toast
Croissants
Marmalade
Honey and preserves

Tea
Coffee

MRS BEETON'S OXFORD SAUSAGES

1.5 kg/3½ lb pork **or** *500 g/18 oz lean pork, 500 g/18 oz veal and 500 g/18 oz beef dripping*
500 g/18 oz soft white breadcrumbs
5 ml /1 tsp ground pepper
grated rind of ½ lemon
grated nutmeg
6 chopped sage leaves
2.5 ml/½ tsp chopped winter savory
2.5 ml/½ tsp marjoram

Choose lean pork, without skin and gristle. Cut it up roughly and mince according to taste; for a fine cut, however, it must be put through the coarse plate first, otherwise it will clog the machine. Mix the rest of the ingredients into the sausagemeat and mince again. Fill the sausagemeat into skins using a sausage-filler, or make it into little cakes or cork shapes. Allow to mature for 12–14 hours in a cool place, to allow flavour and texture to develop.

MAKES 36 SAUSAGES OR 60–70 CHIPOLATAS

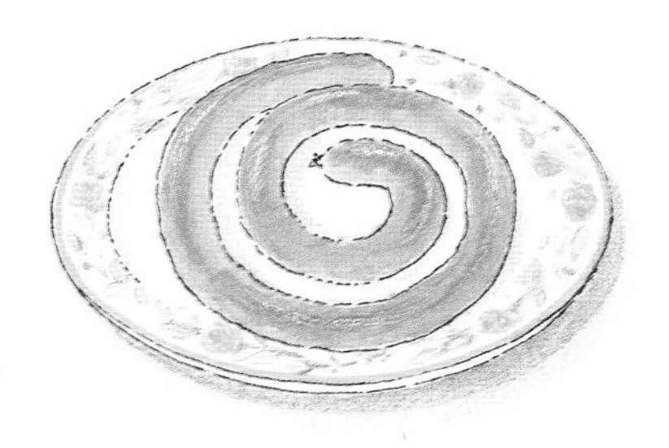

CUMBERLAND SAUSAGE

lard
450 g/1 lb lean shoulder of pork
150 g/5 oz pork fat
1 rasher of smoked bacon, without rind
50 g/2 oz wholemeal breadcrumbs
5 ml/1 tsp salt
2.5 ml/½ tsp pepper
large pinch of ground mace
large pinch of grated nutmeg
1.25 ml/¼ tsp dried thyme (optional)
large pinch of dried crushed sage (optional)

Set the oven at 160°C/325°F/gas 3. Grease a baking sheet with a small amount of lard.

Chop the pork finely or mince it coarsely with the fat and bacon. Mix in the breadcrumbs, and season well with the salt, pepper, spices, and herbs.

Shape or pipe the pork mixture into a long continuous roll about 2.5 cm/1 inch thick and coil up on the sheet like a Catherine wheel. Prick well with a fork, melt some lard, and brush the sausage very lightly with it.

Bake for 30–45 minutes or until the sausage is completely cooked. Drain off the fat, and serve the sausage cut in short lengths.

SERVES 8–10

SERVING A BREAKFAST BUFFET

The most effective and satisfactory way to serve a breakfast buffet is to organize one large or several small tables with individual place settings, and to arrange all the food on a sideboard or side tables. Lay the main table or tables with matching or co-ordinating cloths and decorate with a central vase of delicate flowers – yellows or pinks are good for a morning table – or place individual posies in pretty egg cups or small decorative glasses at each place. Tie rolled napkins with narrow satin ribbons that match the colour scheme, or tuck them into dainty napkin-rings. Have available on each small table, or at several points on a big table, salt and pepper pots, jugs of milk, bowls of sugar and dishes of butter and marmalade. Coffee and tea can be taken round, or a pot of each may be placed on the table. Cover the sideboard with a pretty cloth and at one end place the cereals, fruit compôtes and juices with a supply of small bowls and glasses. Next to them arrange the savoury dishes – hot ones at the back and cold at the front – and alongside, a pile of large plates. At the other end have baskets of bread and dishes of toast, muffins and croissants. If there is room set a vase of flowers or a bowl of fruit in a central position.

BREAKFAST PANCAKES

1 egg
250 ml/8 fl oz milk
30 ml/2 tbsp melted butter **or** *oil*
15 ml/1 tbsp caster sugar
100 g/4 oz plain flour
10 ml/2 tsp baking powder
2.5 ml/½ tsp salt
fat **or** *oil for frying*

Beat the egg until liquid, add the remaining ingredients and whisk to make a smooth batter.

Heat a little melted butter or oil in a frying pan. Pour off any excess.

Put 30 ml/2 tbsp batter into the pan to make a pancake about 10 cm/4 inches in diameter. Bubbles will soon appear on the surface of the pancake.

As soon as it is brown underneath but before the bubbles break, turn the pancake over and cook the other side until brown. Transfer to a clean tea-towel, fold the towel over it, and keep warm.

Cook the remaining batter using the same method, greasing the pan when necessary.

Serve in piles of three with butter and maple syrup or marmalade, or with grilled sausage and bacon.

SERVES 4

FISHY BREAKFASTS

Fish is an excellent source of protein and minerals without containing the fats and cholesterol of eggs, bacon and other meats. Mixed with potatoes to make fishcakes, or with rice to make kedgeree, it gives a nourishing and filling meal. On its own it makes a light but satisfying start to the day.

POACHED OR GRILLED SMOKED HADDOCK

450–575 g/1–1¼ lb smoked haddock fillets
milk
pepper
butter **or** *oil*
parsley butter (optional)

Cut the fins off the fish, and cut it into serving portions if required. To poach, place the fish in one layer in a large frying pan. Add just enough milk, or milk and water mixed, to cover all but the top of the fish. Dust lightly with pepper.

Simmer for 10–15 minutes or until tender. Lift each piece in turn on to a fish slice, drain well, and place on a heated dish or plate.

Brush lightly with butter, and serve topped with a pat of chilled parsley butter if liked.

To grill, place the portions in a large frying pan and cover with boiling water. Leave to stand for 5 minutes.

Lift each piece on to a fish slice, drain well, and place the pieces, skin side up, in the grill pan.

Grill under a medium heat for 3–5 minutes, depending on the thickness of the fish. Turn, brush the fish lightly with butter or oil, dust with pepper, and grill for another 4 minutes or until tender.

Serve topped with pats of chilled parsley butter, if liked.

SERVES 4

FINNAN HADDOCK

Finnan, or Findon, haddock are thought to be the most delicious of all smoked haddocks. They are named after Findon – a hamlet in Kincardineshire, 6 miles south of Aberdeen, and were traditionally dried over the smoke of sea-weed and sprinkled with sea water during the smoking process. The fish acquired a subtle, delicate flavour unlike any other smoked haddock. In more recent times the method has changed slightly. The haddock are soaked in salt water for at least two hours, or overnight, and they are then hung in the open air to dry. They are smoked in a chimney over burning peat or hardwood sawdust. If no chimney is available, open-ended casks are used. The smoking should not go on for more than twelve hours, and at the end of it, the fish should be of a fine yellow colour.

Recipes using smoked haddock often specify the Findon variety, and the most common way to bake it is with rashers of unsmoked bacon or slices of salt pork. In Scotland, the combination of ham and haddie is thought to be as delicious a marriage of flavours as bacon and eggs.

KEDGEREE

150 g/5 oz long-grain rice
400 g/14 oz smoked haddock
100 ml/4 fl oz milk
100 ml/4 fl oz water
50 g/2 oz butter
10 ml/2 tsp curry powder
salt and pepper
cayenne pepper
2 hard-boiled eggs, coarsely chopped

Garnish
15 ml/1 tbsp chopped parsley
butter

Put the rice into a saucepan of boiling water, boil for 12 minutes and drain thoroughly. Keep warm.

Poach the haddock in the milk and water in a covered frying pan for 4 minutes. Remove the fish from the pan and drain. Remove the skin and tail, and break up the fish into fairly large flakes.

Melt half the butter in a saucepan. Blend in the curry powder and add the flaked fish. Warm the mixture through. Warm the rice in the remaining butter.

Season both the fish mixture and the rice with salt, pepper, and a few grains of cayenne pepper. Add the hard-boiled egg to the fish and combine the mixture with the rice.

Pile the mixture on a heated dish and sprinkle with chopped parsley. Dot with butter and serve immediately.

SERVES 4

FISH CAKES

300 g/11 oz cooked white fish
(cod, haddock, coley, etc)
500 g/18 oz cold potatoes
25 g/1 oz butter
30 ml/2 tbsp single cream
15 ml/1 tbsp finely chopped parsley
salt and pepper
flour for coating
butter or oil for shallow-frying

Flake the fish and be sure to remove all the bones carefully.

Mash the potatoes until smooth, and mix in the butter and cream. Add the flaked fish and parsley, and season to taste.

Divide the mixture into eight portions, and shape into flat, round cakes. Season the flour, and dip each cake in it. Shallow-fry in butter or oil for 6–8 minutes, turning once.

SERVES 4

JUGGED OR POACHED KIPPERS

4 kippers
boiling water

Put the kippers, tail ends up, in a tall, heatproof jug. Pour boiling water over the whole fish except the tails. Cover the jug with a cloth, and leave to stand for 5 minutes.

Tilt the jug gently over a sink, and drain off the water. Do not try to pull the kippers out by their tails. Serve them on warmed plates.

SERVES 4

GRILLED KIPPERS

4 kippers
20 ml /4 tsp butter **or** *margarine*

Garnish
4 pats chilled butter
chopped parsley

Lay the kippers flat, skin side up, on the grill pan base (not on the rack). Grill under a medium heat for 3 minutes. Turn, dot each kipper with 5 ml/1 tsp butter or margarine, and grill for another 3 minutes.

Serve on warmed plates, topped with pats of chilled butter and sprinkled with parsley.

SERVES 4

*B*READ

Try some of these recipes as a change from toast. Croissants and brioche are slightly sweet, so are best eaten with butter and preserves, whereas muffins, soda bread and oatmeal pancakes are perfect with a cooked breakfast, or with marmalade, jams, honey or cheeses.

CROISSANTS

400 g/14 oz strong white flour
5 ml/1 tsp salt
100 g/4 oz lard
25 g/1 oz yeast **or**
15 ml/1 tbsp dried yeast
200 ml/7 fl oz warm water
1 egg
flour for dusting
75 g/3 oz unsalted butter
beaten egg for glazing
fat for greasing

Sift the flour and salt into a large bowl. Rub in 25 g/1 oz of the lard.

Blend the fresh yeast into the warm water or reconstitute the dried yeast. Beat the egg until liquid. Stir the egg and yeast liquid into the flour and mix to a soft dough consistency.

Turn on to a lightly floured surface and knead for about 8 minutes or until the dough is smooth and no longer sticky. Put the dough in a large, lightly oiled polythene bag and leave at room temperature for 15 minutes.

Meanwhile, beat together the remaining lard and the butter until well mixed; then chill.

On a lightly floured surface, roll the dough carefully into an oblong measuring 50 × 20 cm/20 × 8 inches. Divide the chilled fat into three equal portions. Use one-third to dot over the top two-thirds of the dough, leaving a small border clear for sealing.

Fold the dough into three by bringing up the plain part of it first, then bringing the top, fat-covered third down over it. Seal the edges together by pressing with the rolling pin.

Give the dough a quarter turn and repeat the rolling and folding twice, using the other two portions of fat. Put the dough in the polythene bag and leave in a cool place for 15 minutes.

Repeat the rolling and folding three more times. Rest the dough in the polythene bag in a cool place for 15 minutes.

Roll it into an oblong measuring about 35 × 25 cm/14 × 10 inches and then cut out six 13 cm/5 inch squares. Cut each square into two triangles.

Brush the surface of the dough with beaten egg and roll each triangle loosely, towards the point, finishing with the tip underneath. Curve into a crescent shape.

Place on a greased baking sheet and brush with beaten egg. Put the baking sheet in the polythene bag again and leave in a warm place for about 30 minutes or until the dough is light and puffy.

Meanwhile, set the oven at 220°C/425°F/gas 7. Bake the croissants for 15–20 minutes until golden brown and crisp.

MAKES 12 CROISSANTS

CONTINENTAL BREAKFAST

Yoghurt
Fruit juice

Omelette paysanne

Croissants
Brioche
Preserves and cheeses

Coffee
Hot chocolate

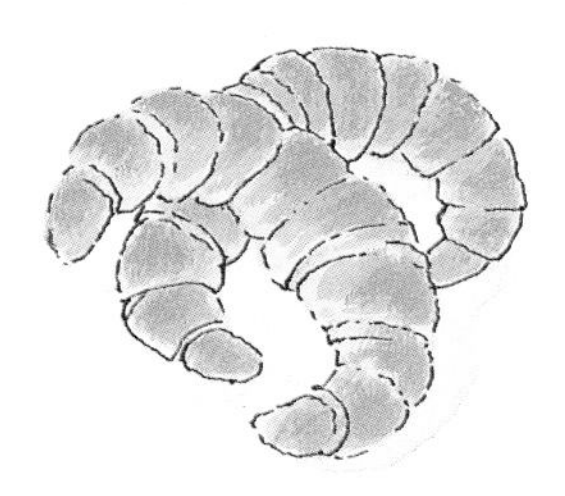

TO MAKE PERFECT TOAST

For dry toast

- Never use new bread. A loaf that is one or two days old is much better.
- Cut neat slices approximately 5 mm (¼ inch) thick and trim off any ragged edges.
- Toast both sides of each slice under a low grill, allowing the bread to dry before browning.
- Be careful not to let the slices become too brown as this will spoil the flavour.
- Make the toast just before it is needed, or it will toughen.

For hot buttered toast

- Cut slices as above, leaving the crust on.
- Toast both sides of each slice under a moderate grill, until a pale golden colour.
- Spread with butter, or a low fat spread, trim-off the crusts and any ragged edges.
- Cut each slice individually into four triangular pieces and arrange on a warmed plate or dish. Serve immediately.

BRIOCHE

400 g/14 oz strong white flour
5 ml/1 tsp salt
10 ml/2 tsp sugar
50 g/2 oz butter
25 g/1 oz fresh yeast **or**
15 ml/1 tbsp dried yeast
40 ml/8 tsp warm water
2 eggs
flour for kneading
fat for greasing
beaten egg for glazing

Sift the flour, salt, and sugar into a large bowl. Rub in the butter. Blend the fresh yeast into the warm water or reconstitute the dried yeast. Beat the eggs into the yeast liquid and stir into the flour to form a soft dough.

Turn on to a floured surface and knead for about 5 minutes or until the dough is smooth and no longer sticky. Put in a large, lightly oiled polythene bag and leave in a warm place for about 45 minutes or until doubled in size.

Grease 22 7.5 cm/3 inch brioche or deep bun tins.

Knead the dough again until firm and cut into 22 equal pieces. Cut off one-quarter of each piece. Form the larger piece into a ball and place in a prepared tin. Firmly press a hole in the centre and place the remaining quarter as a knob in the centre. Put the tins on a baking sheet and cover with the polythene bag. Leave in a warm place for about 30 minutes or until the dough is light and puffy.

Meanwhile, set the oven at 230°C/450°F/gas 8. Brush the brioche with beaten egg and bake for 15–20 minutes until a golden brown colour.

MAKES 22 BRIOCHES

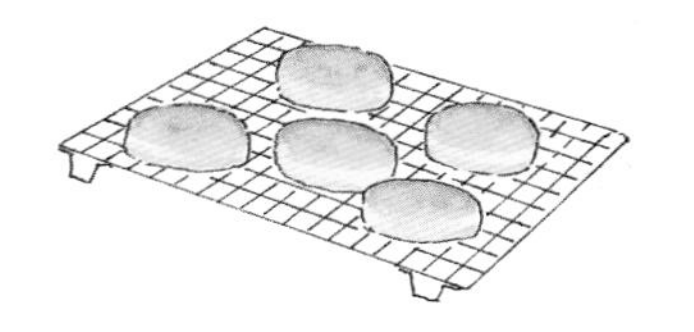

MUFFINS

150 g/5 oz plain flour
5 ml/1 tsp baking powder
2.5 ml/½ tsp salt
50 g/2 oz sugar
100 g/4 oz natural wheat bran
5 ml/1 tsp bicarbonate of soda
200 ml/7 fl oz milk
25 g /1 oz butter
30 ml/2 tbsp golden syrup
1 egg
fat for greasing

Grease 20 5cm/2 inch patty tins. Set the oven at 200°C/400°F/gas 6.

Sift the flour, baking powder, and salt into a large bowl. Add the sugar and bran. Dissolve the bicarbonate of soda in the milk. Melt the butter and syrup together.

Add the milk, syrup and egg to the dry ingredients and mix with a wooden spoon until they are absorbed into a lumpy mixture. Do not over-mix.

Spoon the mixture into the prepared patty tins, filling them only two-thirds full, and bake for about 15–20 minutes or until brown and springy to the touch.

Loosen from the pans with a palette knife. Cool on a wire rack. Serve while still just warm, or cold.

MAKES 20 MUFFINS

HEALTHY BREAKFAST

Fresh fruit compôte
Yoghurt
Muesli

Poached haddock
or
Poached, boiled or coddled eggs

Bran muffins
Low fat spread
Marmalade and honey

Herbal tea
Decaffeinated coffee
Fruit juices

MARMALADE

Two stories are told to explain the origin of the name of our traditional breakfast preserve. One says that Mary Queen of Scots' Spanish doctor concocted cures for her seasickness using oranges and sugar. Mary's French courtiers always knew when 'Marie est malade'. The more probable explanation is that the name derives from the Portuguese word for quince, 'marmelo', from which the first preserves were made with honey or sweet wine.

The first orange marmalade is believed to have been made in Scotland in the eighteenth century by Janet Pierson, wife of the grocer, James Keiller. One day a shipment of oranges arrived from Spain and was being unloaded at the harbour. James could not resist buying a large quantity, but the fruit turned out to be too bitter to eat. So Janet experimented, using recipes she had for quince 'marmalet'. The resulting jam was a great success and the first batch sold out in a few hours. Recipes for orange marmalades quickly started appearing in cookery books and the preserve became firmly established as a British breakfast food.

*B*RUNCHES

Brunch is the ideal meal for a leisurely Sunday morning, when the day stretches out in front of you and there is nothing to hurry for. Invite a few friends and enjoy a real party with Buck's Fizz and any number of delicious savouries.

POTATO BATTER CAKES

100 g/4 oz plain flour
375 ml/13 fl oz milk
1 egg
5–7.5 ml/1–1½ tsp salt
8 potatoes
butter, margarine, lard
or *vegetable oil for frying*

Blend together the flour and milk in a bowl. Beat in the egg and salt to taste to make a pancake batter. Grate the potatoes into the batter, and mix well.

Heat a knob of fat or spoonful of oil in a large, shallow frying pan, and pour in 30 ml/2 tbsp batter for each cake. Spread the mixture thinly, and fry for 4–6 minutes, turning once, until crisp and golden-brown. Drain on absorbent kitchen paper.

Serve with fried bacon or sausages, or with cranberry sauce.

SERVES 4

OATMEAL PANCAKES

about 300 ml/½ pint milk
15 g/½ oz fresh yeast
200 g/7 oz plain flour
75 g/3 oz fine oatmeal
2.5 ml/½ tsp salt
1 egg
pork rind **or** *oil for greasing*
butter (optional)

Warm 125 ml/4½ fl oz of the milk to hand-hot and blend the yeast into 30 ml/2 tbsp of it. Leave for 10 minutes until frothy.

Sift the flour into a large bowl, then mix in the oatmeal and salt. Work in the yeast mixture. Beat the egg lightly and add it.

Add the warmed milk to the remaining cold milk and heat until tepid; then add enough to the flour mixture to make a smooth batter of slow dropping consistency.

Put the mixing bowl in a large, lightly oiled polythene bag, and leave in a fairly warm place for about 30 minutes to rise. Check the consistency; if thick, add more warm milk gradually to obtain a batter of dropping consistency. Leave for another 30 minutes.

Heat a lightly greased round griddle (Welsh bakestone) or heavy frying pan. Drop heaped spoonfuls of batter on the hot surface, and fry until lightly browned on each side, turning once.

Spread the butter and eat hot. Alternatively, cool, store in an airtight tin, and reheat gently when required.

MAKES ABOUT 20 PANCAKES

KIDNEYS AND SCRAMBLED EGGS

3 small calf's kidneys **or** *4 lamb's kidneys*
salt and pepper
1 small onion, finely chopped
100 g/4 oz butter
60 ml/4 tbsp sherry (optional)
5–6 eggs
125 ml/4½ fl oz milk

Garnish
finely diced sweet red pepper
30 ml/2 tbsp chopped parsley

Skin the kidneys, cut them in half lengthways, and remove the cores; then slice them very thinly. Season to taste.

Melt 25 g/1 oz of the butter in a pan, add the onion, and fry it lightly until golden.

Add the kidneys, and fry quickly, stirring all the time or shaking the pan well, until browned lightly all over. Pour off any excess fat.

Remove the kidneys, arrange them in a circle on a warmed serving dish, and keep hot.

Beat the eggs until liquid, add the milk, and season to taste.

Heat the remaining butter in a pan, and scramble the eggs gently until the mixture starts to thicken.

Pile the scrambled eggs in the centre of the circle of kidneys. Garnish with red pepper and chopped parsley, and serve at once.

SERVES 6

BACON AND EGG OMELETTE

250 g/9 oz back bacon rashers, without rinds
15 ml/1 tbsp plain flour
90 ml/3½ fl oz milk
4 eggs
salt and pepper
15 g/½ oz butter
Garnish
chopped parsley **or** *chives*
tomato wedges

Place the bacon in the grill pan, and cook under a moderate heat for 3–4 minutes until golden brown and crisp.

Meanwhile, blend the flour and milk. Beat in the eggs, and season to taste.

Melt the butter in a frying pan, and heat until just turning brown. Pour in the egg mixture, and cook for 5–6 minutes over a fairly high heat until set, lifting the edges occasionally.

Place the hot bacon rashers on top. Garnish with chopped parsley or chives, and wedges of tomato. Serve from the pan.

SERVES 3–4

BRUNCH

Bucks Fizz
Dried fruit compôte

Scrambled eggs with smoked salmon
Kedgeree
Mushrooms
Bacon
Grilled kidneys
Sausages
Potato batter cakes

Irish soda bread
Bran muffins
Croissants
Marmalade, honey, preserves and cheeses

Tea
Coffee
Hot chocolate

OMELETTE ARNOLD BENNETT

150 g/5 oz smoked haddock
30 ml/2 tbsp clarified **or** *unsalted butter*
50 ml/2 fl oz single cream
2 eggs
salt and pepper
30 ml/2 tbsp grated Parmesan cheese

Put the haddock in a frying pan, cover with water and poach for 10 minutes. Drain, remove any skin or bones, and flake the flesh into a bowl. Add 15 ml/1 tbsp of the butter and 15 ml/1 tbsp of the cream. Mix well together.

Separate the eggs. Beat the yolks with 5 ml/1 tsp cream and season to taste. Mix together the yolks, haddock, and half the cheese. Whisk the egg whites until stiff, and fold them into the mixture.

Heat half the remaining butter in an omelette pan. Heat the grill. Pour half the mixture into the hot pan and cook quickly until golden.

Sprinkle over half the remaining cheese, spoon over 15 ml/1 tbsp cream, and brown quickly under the grill. Do not fold. Serve immediately.

SERVES 2

HAM AND HADDIE

575 g/1¼ lb finnan haddock on the bone
125 ml/4½ fl oz milk
25 g/1 oz butter
4 slices cooked ham
(about 125 g/4½ oz each)
salt
freshly ground black pepper
50 ml/2 fl oz double cream

Put the haddock in a large frying pan and add the milk. Bring to the boil and simmer for 10–20 minutes until the fish is cooked.

Remove the fish from the pan. Strain the liquid and reserve it. Skin, bone, and flake the fish.

Heat the butter in a clean frying pan and add the ham slices; heat through, turning once. Place the fish on the ham and pour the liquid over them. Season with salt and freshly ground black pepper and pour the cream over the fish. Brown quickly under a hot grill before serving.

SERVES 4

HUNT BREAKFASTS

Hunting was a favourite Victorian pastime, and etiquette required the host of each hunt to provide a plentiful meal for his guests before the hunt began. The hunt breakfast usually began at about 9.30 am and was held in the dining-room, the billiard-room or the great hall. There was a vast array of cold meats – beef, pheasant, hams, game, chicken and turkey – as well as hot dishes of eggs, chops and kidneys. There were also piles of hot buttered muffins, large loaves of bread and great quantities of cheese. The ladies were usually served sherry and light refreshments while the gentlemen tucked into the main meal and drank brandy, cherry brandy, liqueurs, ale or champagne. After this vast breakfast, the meet assembled, and stirrup cups, containing a mixture of port and cherry brandy or ginger wine, were passed around before the hunt got under way.